Pink Floyd

Play Along with 9 Great-Sounding ...

T0040755

To access audio visit:
www.halleonard.com/mylibrary

Enter Code
7304-2133-2615-3114

HAL•LEONARD® CORPORATION

7777 W. BLUEMOUND RD. P.O. BOX 13819 MILWAUKEE, WI 53213

ISBN 978-0-7390-5044-6

Recorded at the Mews Recording Studios, London
www.themewsrecordingstudios.com
Dave Clarke, recording and mix engineer
Tom Fleming, guitars
Neil Williams, bass
Darrin Mooney, drums
Alle Pearse, keyboards
Stephen Wilcox, sax
Alison Symons, voice
Children from Gallions School, Newham, choir

Compiled by Matt Smith, Tom Fleming, and Olly Weeks
Book edited by Lucy Holliday and Olly Weeks
Music arranged and engraved by Tom Fleming

Cover photo: © Michael Ochs Archives/Getty Images

Pink Floyd

Play Along with 9 Great-Sounding Tracks

Contents

SEE EMILY PLAY

Words and Music by SYD BARRETT

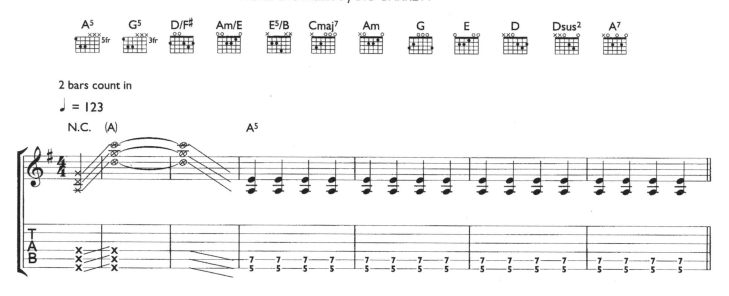

2 bars count in

♩ = 123

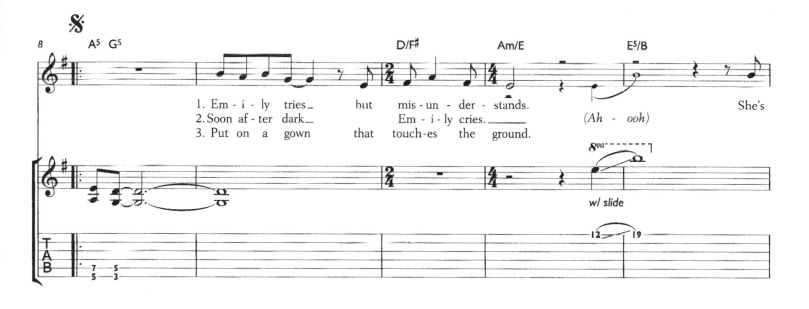

1. Em - i - ly tries___ but mis - un - der - stands.
2. Soon af - ter dark___ Em - i - ly cries.___
3. Put on a gown that touch - es the ground.

(Ah - ooh)

She's

w/ slide

oft - en in - clined___ to bor - row some - bo - dy's dreams___ 'til to - mor - row.___
Gaz - ing through trees___ in sor - row, hard - ly a sound___ 'til to - mor - row.___
Float on a riv - er for - ev - er and ev - er,___ Em - i - ly.___

There is no

(3° play 8va higher)

w/delay

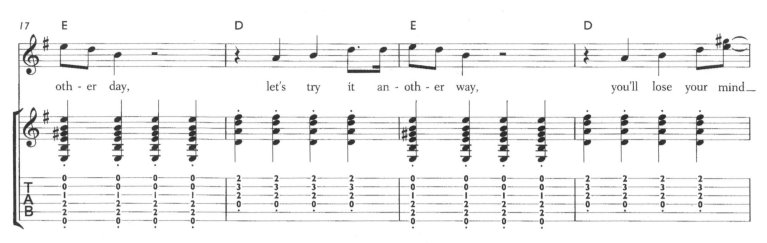

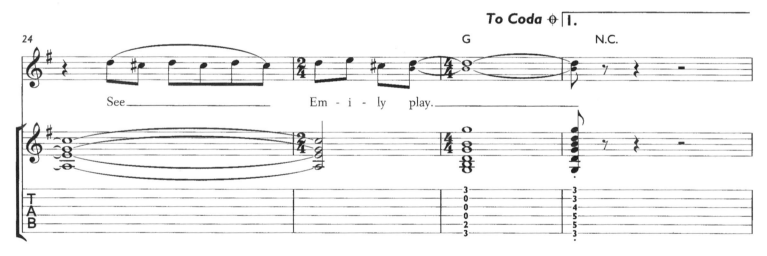

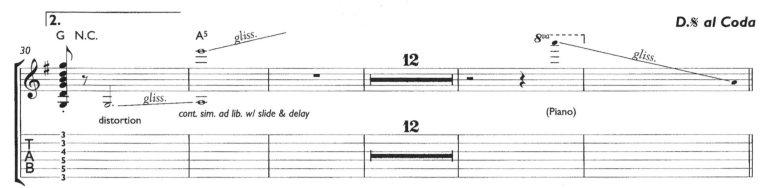

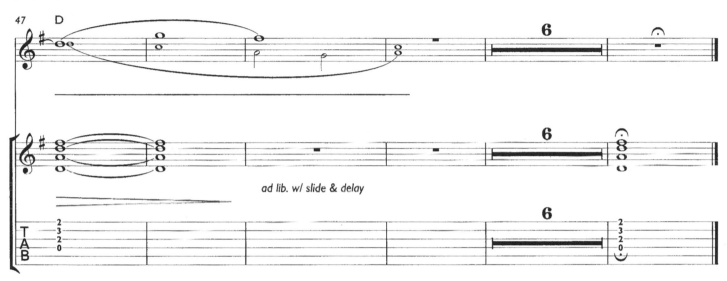

Insert 1 - Recorded by Syd Barrett, Rick Wright and Nick Mason.
The tape was then played at double speed and inserted into the two bars at the end of verse 1.

TIME

Words and Music by ROGER WATERS, NICHOLAS MASON,
DAVID GILMOUR and RICK WRIGHT

there is time to kill — to - day. —
half a page of scrib - bled lines. —

And then one day you find —
Hang - ing on in qui - et

ten years have got — be - hind — you.
des - per - a - tion is the Eng - lish way, — the

To Coda ⊕

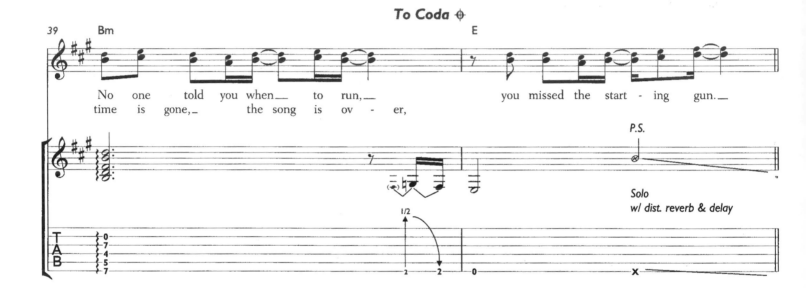

No one told you when — to run, —
time is gone, — the song is ov - er,

you missed the start - ing gun. —

P.S.

Solo
w/ dist. reverb & delay

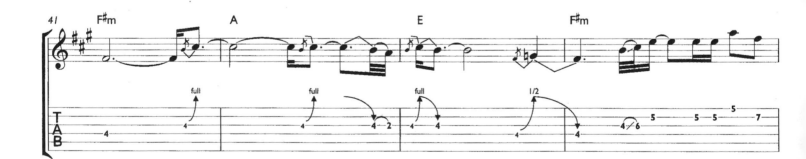

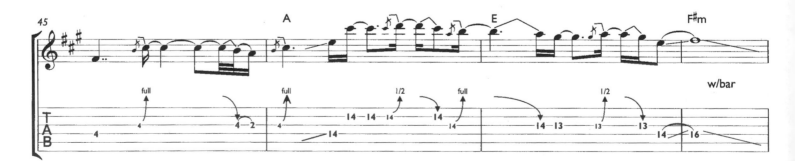

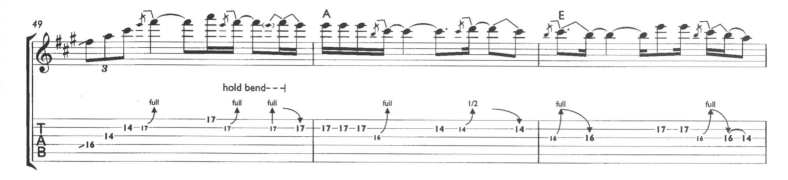

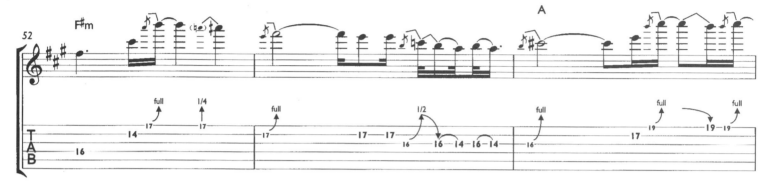

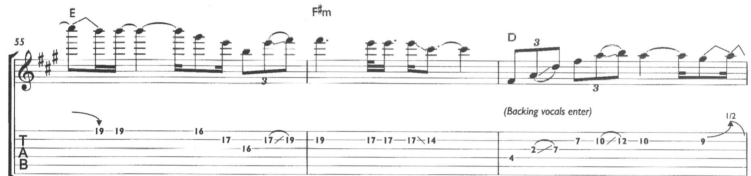

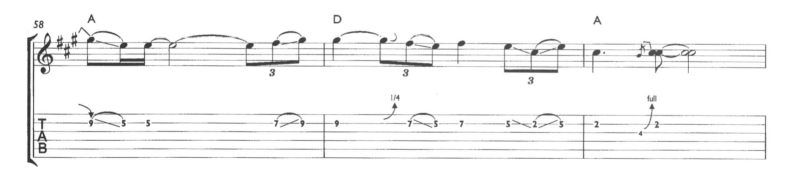

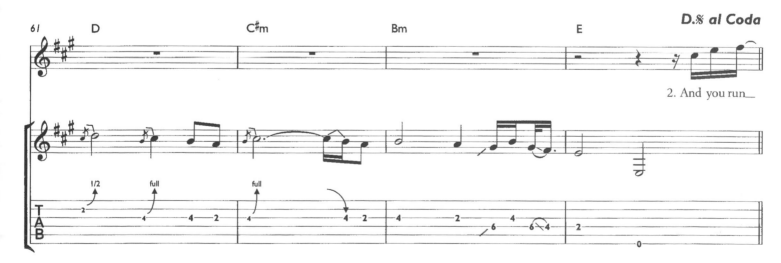

Time - 6 - 4
29150

⊕ **Coda**

Slightly swung sixteenths ♩ = 61

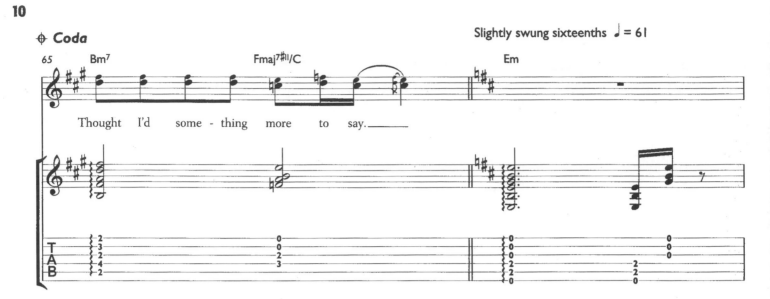

Thought I'd some - thing more to say.___

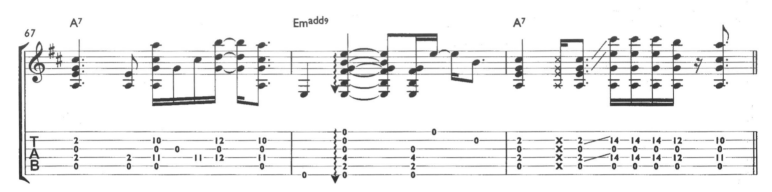

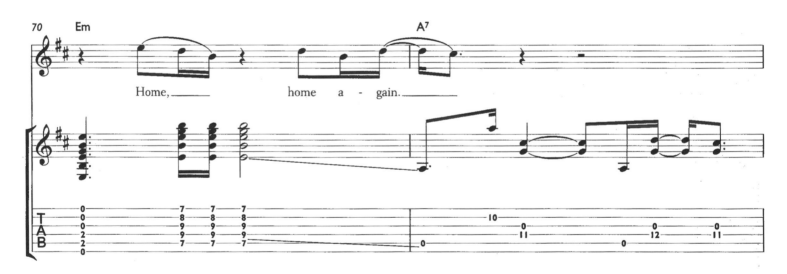

Home,___ home a - gain.

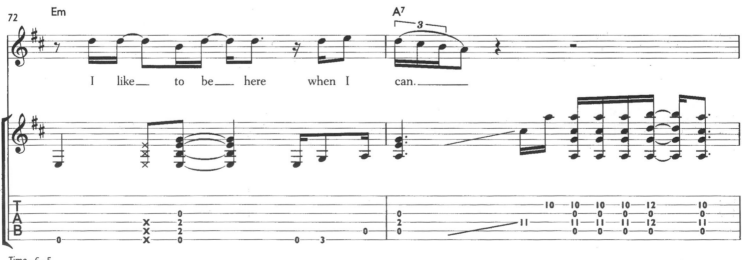

I like___ to be___ here when I can.

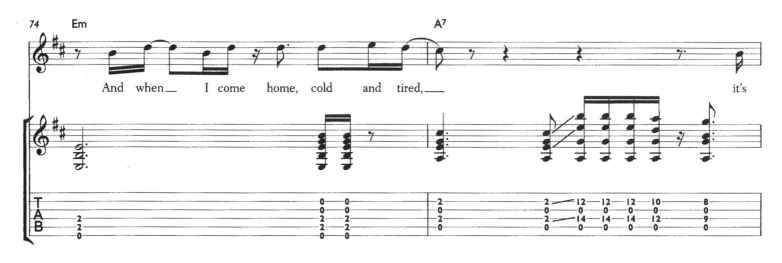

And when__ I come home, cold and tired,__ it's

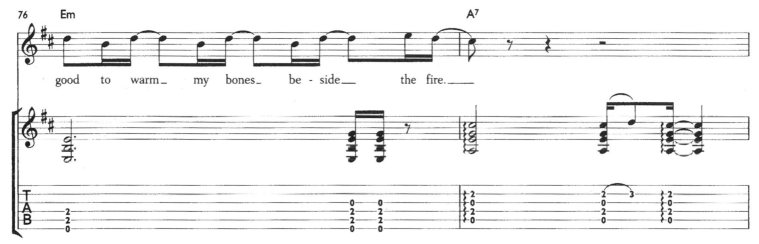

good to warm__ my bones__ be - side__ the fire.__

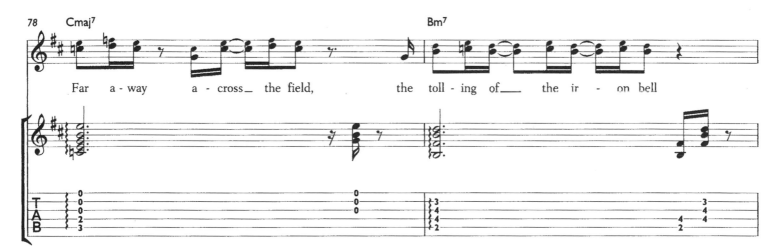

Far a - way a - cross__ the field, the toll - ing of__ the ir - on bell

calls the faith - ful to__ their knees to hear the soft - ly spok - en mag - ic spells.

MONEY
Words and Music by ROGER WATERS

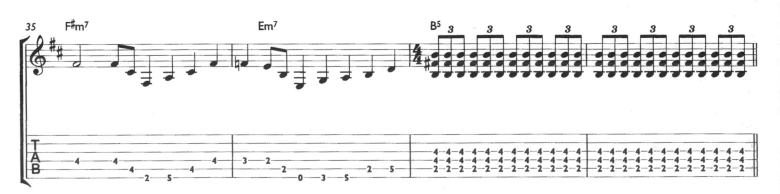

*This solo was originally played on a 24-fret guitar but can be played on 22 frets.

HAVE A CIGAR

Words and Music by ROGER WATERS

Have a Cigar - 9 - 1
29150

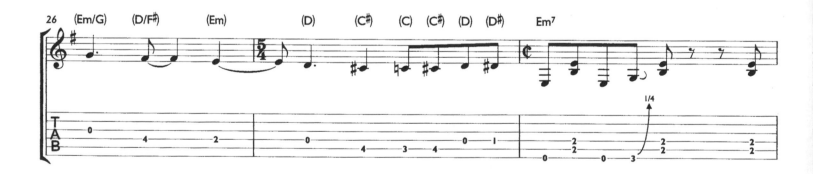

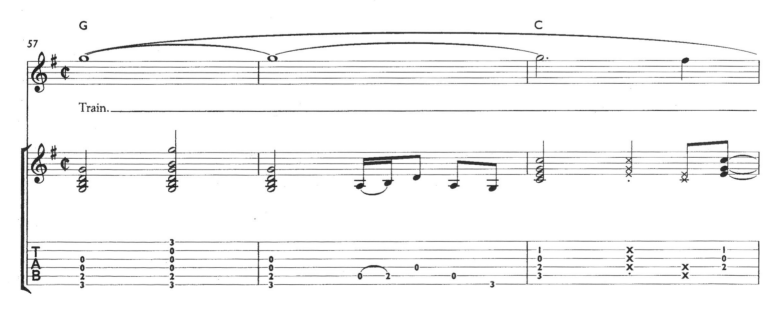

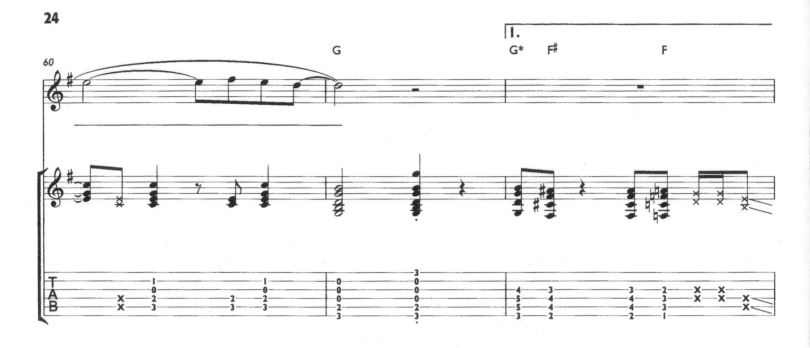

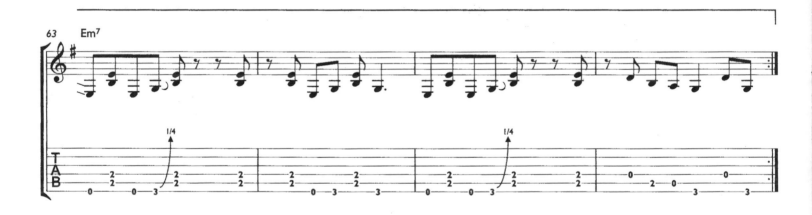

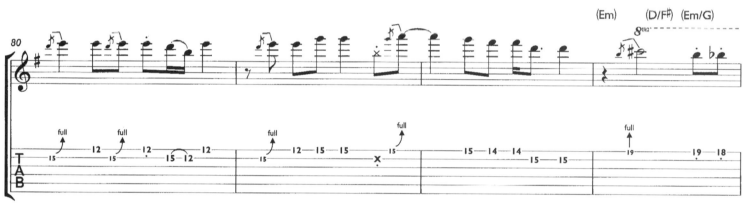

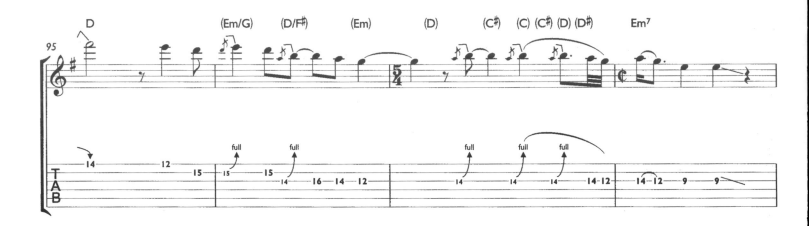

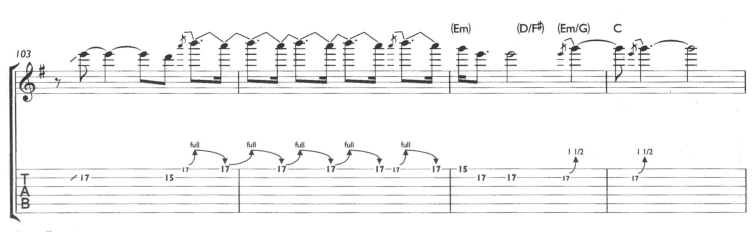

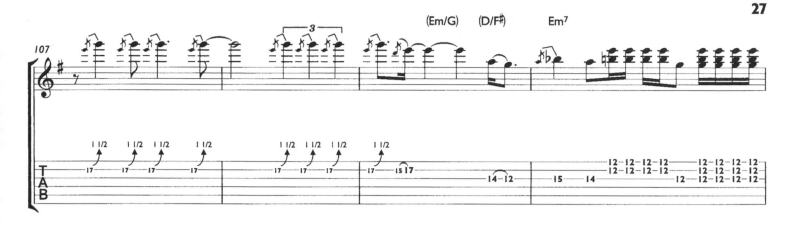

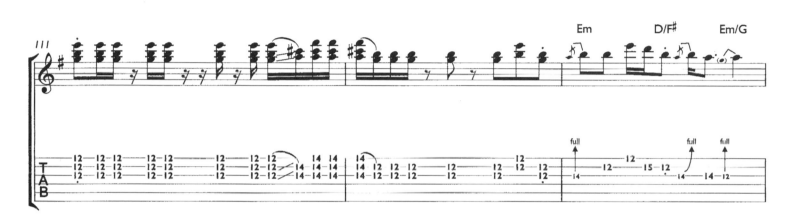

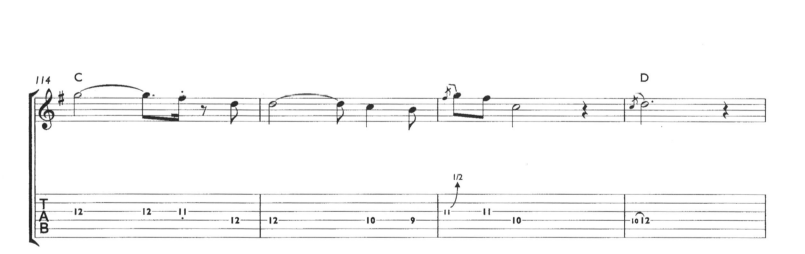

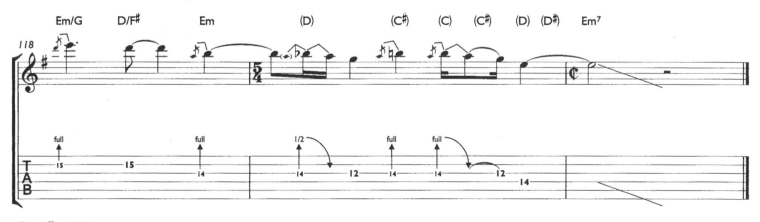

Have a Cigar - 9 - 9
29150

WISH YOU WERE HERE

Words and Music by ROGER WATERS and DAVID GILMOUR

How I wish, how I wish you were here.

We're just two lost souls swim-ming in a fish bowl,— year af-ter year.—

Run-ning ov-er the same old ground, what have we found?— The same old fears?— Wish you were here.—

Wish You Were Here - 5 - 4
29150

Acoustic Guitar & Vocal Scat in cue notes
w/slide & open G tuning

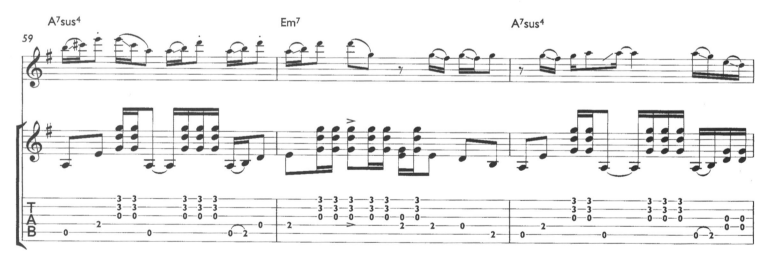

YOUNG LUST

Words and Music by ROGER WATERS and DAVID GILMOUR

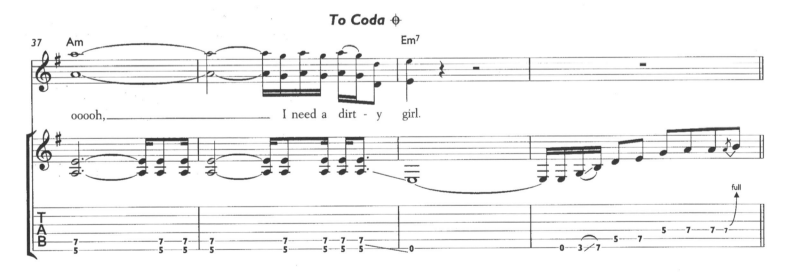

Young Lust - 5 - 3
29150

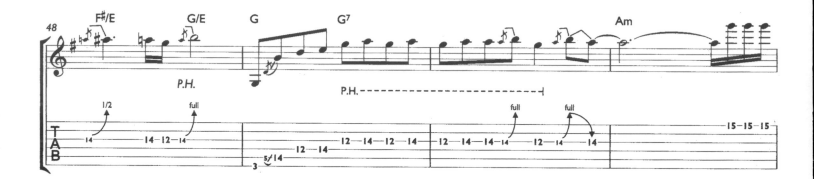

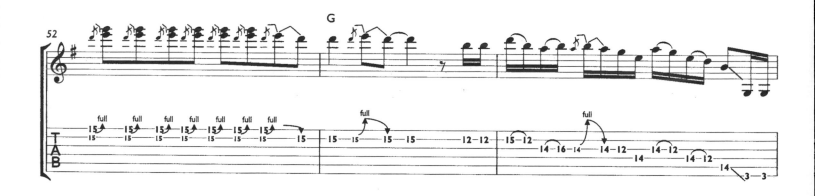

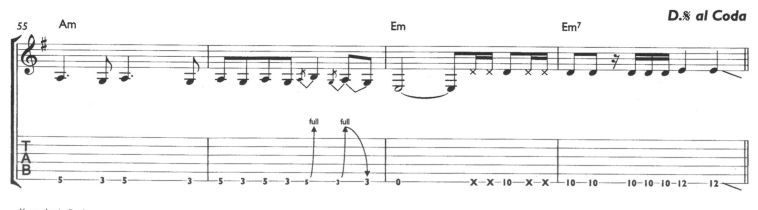

ANOTHER BRICK IN THE WALL
(Part 2)

Words and Music by ROGER WATERS

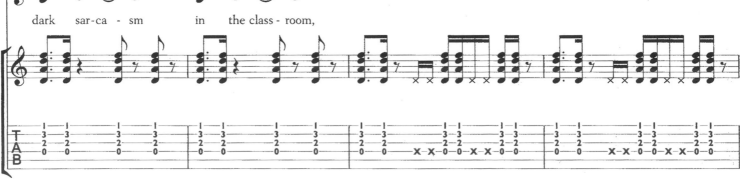

Another Brick in the Wall (Part 2) - 4 - 1
29150

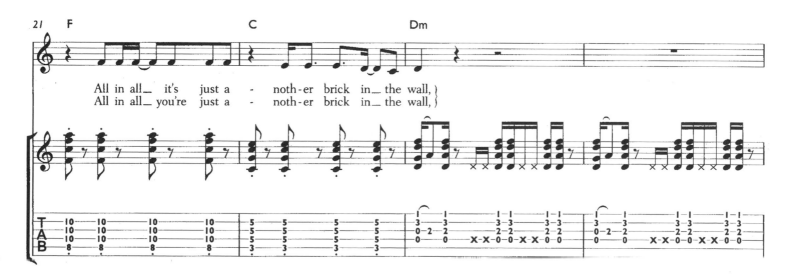

Another Brick in the Wall (Part 2) - 4 - 2
29150

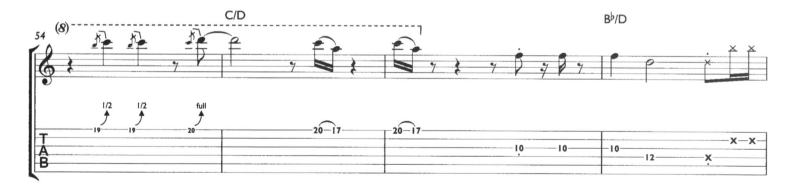

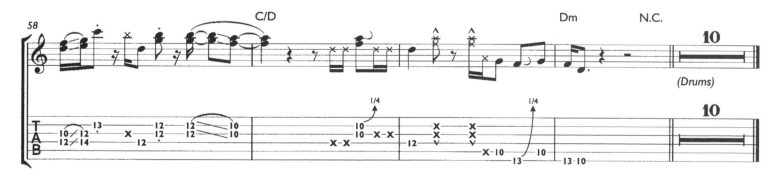

Another Brick in the Wall (Part 2) - 4 - 4
29150

COMFORTABLY NUMB

Words and Music by ROGER WATERS and DAVID GILMOUR

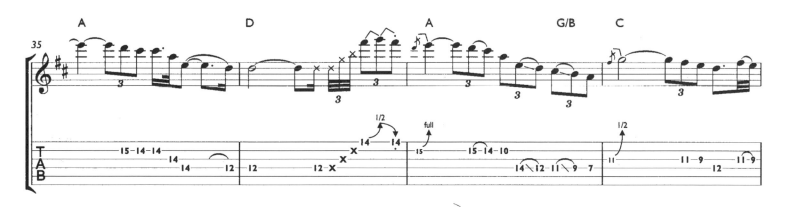

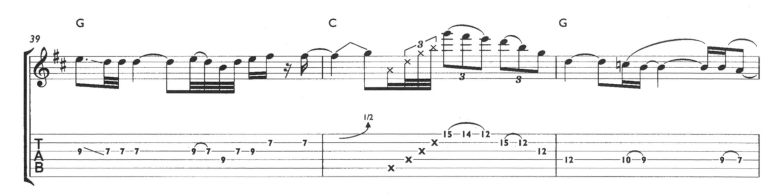

Comfortably Numb - 5 - 2
29150

44

Comfortably Numb - 5 - 3
29150

Comfortably Numb - 5 - 4
29150

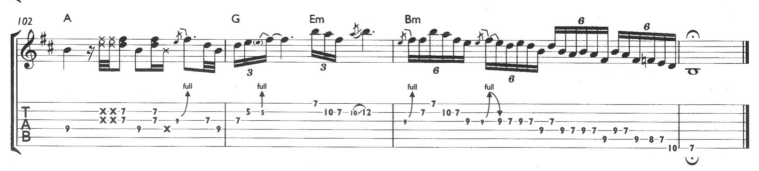

THE FLETCHER MEMORIAL HOME

Words and Music by ROGER WATERS

The Fletcher Memorial Home - 3 - 1
29150

30 Cmaj7

Mr. Brezhnev and party,   *the ghost of McCarthy*

32   D   D7/F#

and the memories of Nixon.   *And now, adding colour,*

34 G   D/F#   C

a group of anonymous Latin American meat packing glitterati."

36 Em   D   G   D/F#

Did they ex-pect us to treat___ them with an-y res-pect?   They can pol-ish their med-als   and

41 C   G   D/F#   C

sharp-en their smiles,___   and a-muse them-selves,   play-ing games for a while.

44 G   D/F#   C   Esus2

Boom boom,   bang bang,   lie down, you're dead.___

47

Solo
w/ dist. & chorus

51   D/F#   G   D/F#   Em7

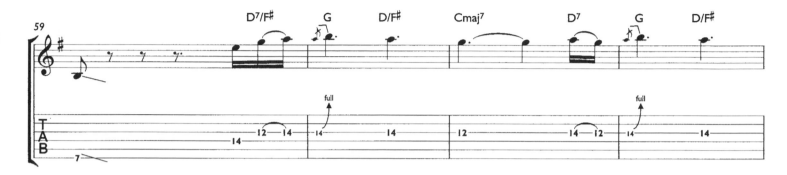

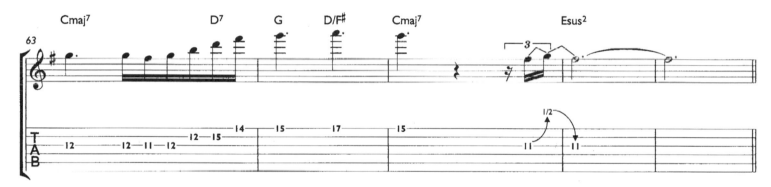

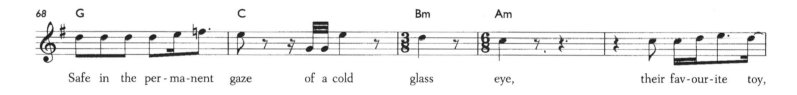

Safe in the per-ma-nent gaze   of a cold   glass   eye,   their fav-our-ite   toy,

— they'll be good girls and boys___   in the Flet-cher Mem or - i - al

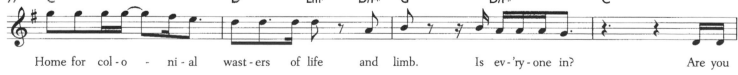

Home for col-o - ni - al   wast-ers of life   and   limb.   Is ev-'ry-one in?   Are you

hav-ing   a nice   time?   Now the fin-al___ sol - u - tion   can be ap-plied.

The Fletcher Memorial Home - 3 - 3
29150

Guitar TAB Guide

Understanding Chord Boxes

Chord boxes show the neck of your guitar as if viewed head on—the vertical lines represent the strings (low E to high E, from left to right), and the horizontal lines represent the frets.

An X above a string means "don't play this string."

An O above a string means "play this open string."

The black dots show you where to put your fingers.

A curved line joining two dots on the fretboard represents a "barre." This means that you flatten one of your fingers (usually the first) so that you hold down all the strings between the two dots at the fret marked.

A fret marking at the side of the chord box shows you where chords that are played higher up the neck are located.

Tuning Your Guitar

The best way to tune your guitar is to use an electronic tuner. Alternatively, you can use relative tuning; this will ensure that your guitar is in tune with itself but won't guarantee that you will be in tune with the original track (or other musicians).

How to Use Relative Tuning

Fret the low E string at the 5th fret and pick the note; compare this with the sound of the open A string. The two notes should be in tune. If not, adjust the tuning of the A string until the two notes match.

Repeat this process for the other strings according to the diagram on the right:

Note that the B string should match the note at the 4th fret of the G string, whereas all the other strings match the note at the 5th fret of the string below.

As a final check, ensure that the bottom E string and top E string are in tune with each other.

E A D G B E

5th fret

Detuning and Capo Use

If the song uses an unconventional tuning, it will say so clearly at the top of the music (for example, "6 = D" [tune the sixth string to D]) or "tune down a whole step." If a capo is used, it will tell you the fret number to which it must be attached. The standard notation will always be in the key at which the song sounds, but the guitar TAB will take tuning changes into account. Just detune/add the capo and follow the fret numbers. The chord symbols will show the sounding chord above and the chord you actually play below in brackets.

Use of Figures

Figures that occur several times in a song will be numbered (e.g., "Fig. 1," "Fig. 2," etc.) A dotted line underneath shows the extent of the "figure." When a phrase is to be played, it will be marked clearly in the score, along with the instrument that should play it.

Reading Guitar Tablature (TAB)

Guitar tablature, or TAB, illustrates the six strings of the guitar graphically, showing you where to put your fingers for each note or chord. TAB is usually shown with standard musical notation above it. The guitar TAB staff has six lines, each of them representing a different string. The top line is the high E string, the second line is the B string, and so on. Instead of using note heads, TAB uses numbers which show the fret number to be played by the left hand. The rhythm is indicated underneath the TAB staff. Ex. 1 (below) shows four examples of single notes.

Ex. 2 shows four different chords. The 3rd one (Asus4) should be played as a barre chord at the 5th fret. For the 4th chord (C9), you have to mute the string marked with an "x" (the A string, in this case) with a finger of your fretting hand in order to obtain the correct voicing.

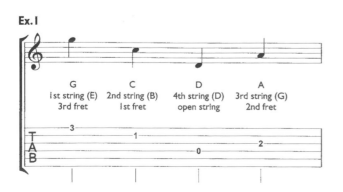

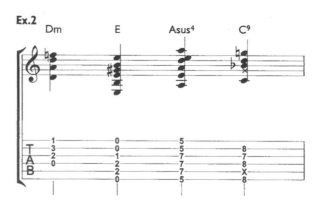

Picking Hand Techniques

1. Down and Up Strokes
These symbols [⊓∨] show that some notes are to be played with a down stroke of the pick and others with up strokes.

2. Palm Mute
"P.M." indicates that you need to mute the notes with the palm of the picking hand by lightly touching the strings near the bridge.

3. Pick Rake
Drag the pick across the indicated strings with a single sweep. The extra pressure will often mute the notes slightly and accentuate the final note.

4. Arpeggiated Chords
Strum across the indicated strings in the direction of the arrow head of the wavy line.

5. Tremolo Picking
Tremolo picking is shown by the slashes on the stem of the note. This is a very fast alternate picking technique. Rapidly and continuously move the pick up and down on each note.

6. Pick Scrape
Drag the edge of the pick up or down the lower strings to create a scraping sound.

7. Right Hand Tapping
"Tap" onto the note indicated by a + with a finger of the picking hand. It is nearly always followed by a pull-off to sound the note fretted below.

8. Tap Slide
The tapped note is slid randomly up the fretboard, then pulled off to the following note.

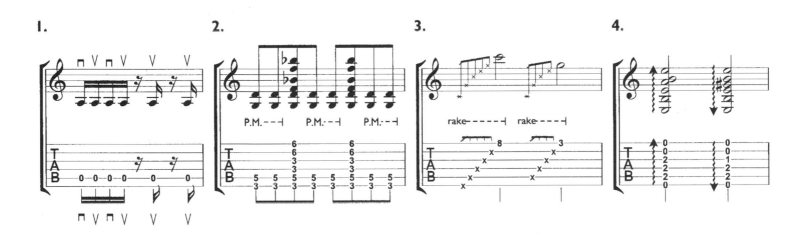

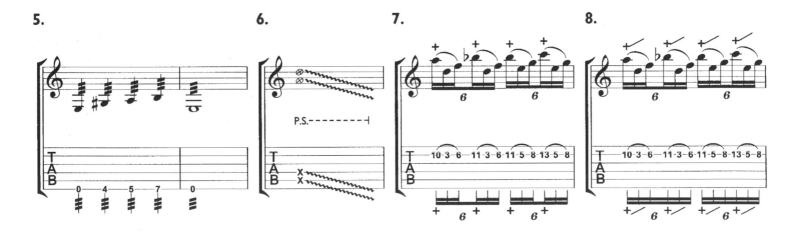

Fretting Hand Techniques

1. Hammer-on and Pull-off
These consist of two or more notes linked together by a slur. For hammer-ons, fret and play the lower note, then "hammer on" to the higher note with another finger. For a pull-off, play the higher note, then "pull off" to a lower note fretted with another finger. In both cases, only pick the first note.

2. Glissandi (Slides)
Fret and pick the first note, then slide the finger up to the second note. If they are slurred together, do not re-pick the second note.

3. Slow Glissando
Play the note(s) and slowly slide the finger(s) in the direction of the diagonal line(s).

4. Quick Glissando
Play the note(s) and immediately slide the finger(s) in the direction of the diagonal line(s).

5. Trills
Play the note and rapidly alternate between this note and the nearest one above in the key. If a note in brackets is shown before, begin with this note.

6. Fret-Hand Muting
Mute the notes with "X" with the fretting hand.

7. Left-Hand Tapping
Sound the note by tapping or hammering on to the note indicated by a [∘] with a finger of the fretting hand.

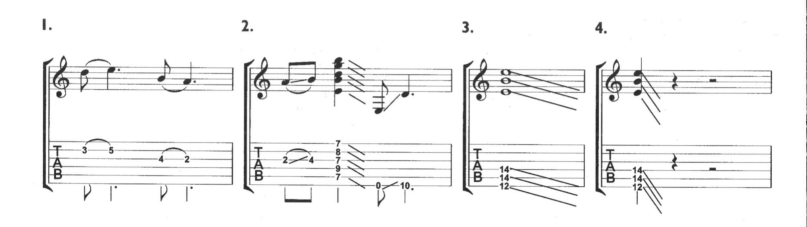

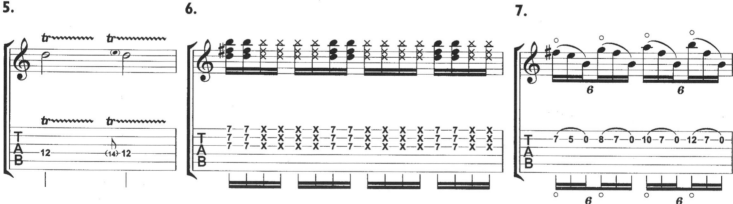

Bends and Vibrato

Bends

Bends are shown by the curved arrow pointing to a number (in the TAB).
Fret the first note and then bend the string up by the value of steps shown.

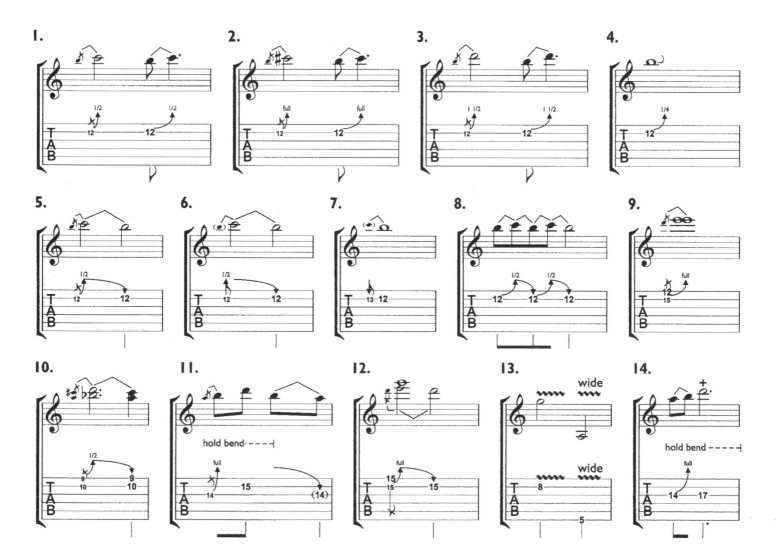

1. Half-Step Bend
The smallest conventional interval; equivalent to raising the note by one fret.

2. Whole-Step Bend
Equivalent to two frets.

3. Whole-Step-and-a-Half Bend
Equivalent to three frets.

4. Quarter-Step Bend
Bend by a slight degree, roughly equivalent to half a fret.

5. Bend and Release
Fret and pick the first note. Bend up for the length of the note shown. Follow with a release of the bend—letting the string fall back down to the original pitch.

6. Ghost Bend (Pre Bend)
Fret the bracketed note and bend quickly before picking the note.

7. Reverse Bend
Fret the bracketed note and bend quickly before picking the note, immediately let it fall back to the original.

8. Multiple Bends
A series of bends and releases joined together. Only pick the first note.

9. Unison Bend
Strike two indicated notes simultaneously and immediately bend the lower string up to the same pitch as the higher one.

10. Double-Note Bend
Play both notes and bend simultaneously by the value shown.

11. Bend Involving More Than One Note
Bend first note and hold the bend while striking a note on another string,

12. Bend Involving Stationary Notes
Play notes and bend lower string. Hold until release is indicated.

13. Vibrato
Shown by a wavy line. The fretting hand creates a vibrato effect using small, rapid up-and-down bends.

14. Bend and Tap Technique
Play and bend notes as shown, then sound the final pitch by tapping onto note as indicated (by + symbol).

Tremolo Arm (Whammy Bar)

1. Vibrato with Tremolo Arm
Create vibrato using small, rapid inflections of the tremolo arm.

2. Tremolo Arm Dive and Return
Play note and depress tremolo arm by degree shown. Release arm to return to original note.

3. Tremolo Arm Scoop
Depress the arm just before picking the note and release.

4. Tremolo Arm Dip
Pick the note, then lower the arm and quickly release.

5. Sustained Note and Dive Bomb
Play the note, hold for length of time shown and then depress arm to lower the pitch until the strings go slack.

6. Flutter
Pick the note and flick the tremolo arm rapidly with the same hand, making the pitch quiver.

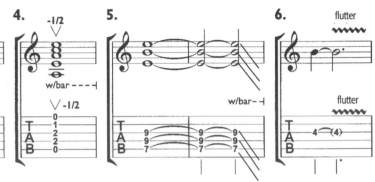
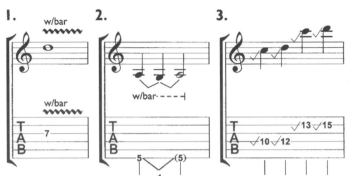

Harmonics and Other Techniques

1. Natural Harmonics
Instead of fretting normally, touch the string lightly with the fretting hand at the fret shown in the TAB. Pick as normal. Diamond noteheads show the resultant pitch.

2. Artificial Harmonics
The first TAB number is fretted and held with the fretting hand as normal. The picking hand then produces a harmonic by using a finger to touch the string lightly at the fret shown by the bracketed number. Pick with another finger of the picking hand.

3. Pinched Harmonics
Fret the note as shown, then create a harmonic by digging into the string with the side of the thumb as you pick.

4. Tapped Harmonics
Fret the note as shown, then create a harmonic by tapping lightly with the picking hand at the fret shown in brackets.

5. Touch Harmonics
Fret the first note, hold it, then touch the string lightly at the fret shown at the end of the slur with the picking hand.

6. Violining
Turn the volume control to zero, pick the notes and then turn the control to fade the note in slowly.

7. Left-Hand Fingering
Small numbers show the finger with which each note is to be fretted.

8. Fingerpicking Notation (PIMA)
Notation that shows which finger should be used to pick each note when playing fingerstyle: p = thumb, i = index, m = middle, a = ring.

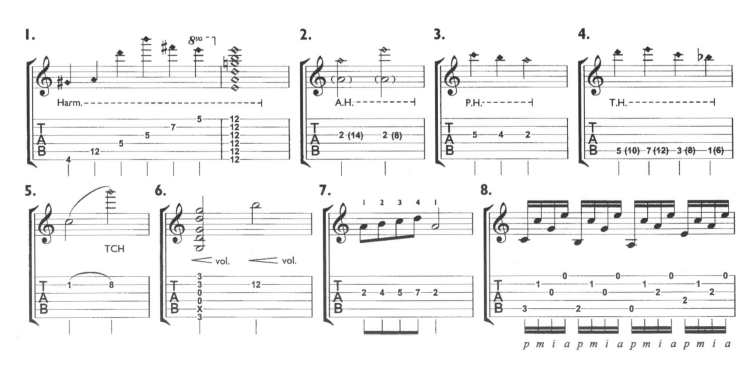

This series will help you play your favorite songs quickly and easily. Just follow the tab and listen to the audio to the hear how the guitar should sound, and then play along using the separate backing tracks. Mac or PC users can also slow down the tempo without changing pitch by using the CD in their computer. The melody and lyrics are included in the book so that you can sing or simply follow along.

INCLUDES TAB

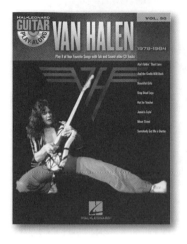  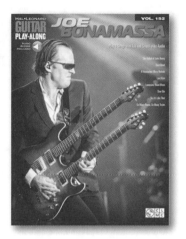 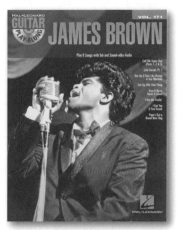

Complete series list and song lists available online.

Prices, contents, and availability subject to change without notice.

HAL•LEONARD® CORPORATION

7777 W. BLUEMOUND RD. P.O. BOX 13819 MILWAUKEE, WI 53213

www.halleonard.com

0615